Basketball
Man-to-Man Defense

By Bill Van Gundy

HIGH
interest
books

Children's Press
A Division of Grolier Publishing
New York / London / Hong Kong / Sydney
Danbury, Connecticut

To Cin, Stan, and Jeff, for no matter what, always supporting and believing in me.

Book Design: Kim M. Sonsky
Contributing Editors: Mark Beyer and Claudia Isler

Photo Credits: Cover, pp. 7, 14, 18, 26, 37, 38, 39 by Thaddeus Harden; p. 15 © Jonathan Daniel/All Sport USA; pp. 10, 24, 29, 30 (both), 34, 36 (both) by Debbie Moyer; p. 32 ©Michael Zito/SportsChrome; p. 40 © Jeff Carlick/SportsChrome.

Special thanks to the Birch Wathen School for use of their facilities during the production of this book.

Visit Children's Press on the Internet at:
http://publishing.grolier.com

Library of Congress Cataloging-in-Publication Data

Van Gundy, Bill.
  Basketball : man-to-man defense / by Bill Van Gundy.
    p. cm.—(Sports clinic)
  Includes bibliographical references and index.
  Summary: Instructions and photographs show how to execute various defensive moves in
      basketball, discussing defensive transition, defending on the ball, defending away from
      the ball, and defending the low post.
  ISBN 0-516-23362-9 (lib. bdg.)—ISBN 0-516-23562-1 (pbk.)
  1. Basketball—Defense—United States—Juvenile literature. [1. Basketball—Defense.] I.
      Title. II. Series.
GV888 .V25 2000

99-058213

CONTENTS

INTRODUCTION

Playing good basketball defense might not get you on TV. However, playing good defense will get you chosen quickly in pickup games. It will also help you to make your school's team. You will gain the respect of other players. In 1988, Michael Jordan said he was happier about winning the Defensive Player of the Year award than being named the NBA's Most Valuable Player.

Man-to-man defense is played not only in pickup and youth league games. It is also played at the game's highest levels: NBA and NCAA Division I. Each defensive player guards one player on the offensive team. This offensive player is the "man" in man-to-man defense. The defender is expected to keep his man from scoring, help teammates, and rebound missed shots. In zone defenses, a defender stays in one area near the basket. He defends only those

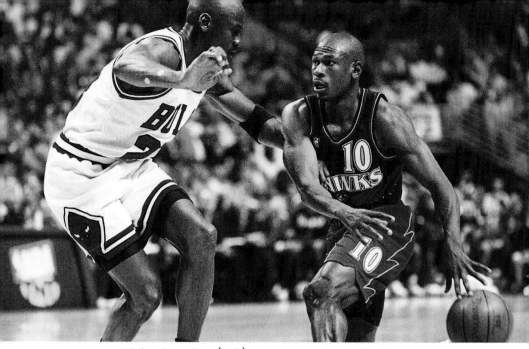
Michael Jordan (left) was as good a defender as
he was at scoring baskets.

opponents coming into that zone. Zone defenses
don't allow defenders to move from their zones.

I coached basketball for forty years. I first coached
high school basketball. Then I coached college basketball. At both of these playing levels, my teams
played only man-to-man defense. I hate zones! Zones
make a player lazy. Zones take away a player's need to
do more on the basketball court. Zone defense makes
rebounding more difficult. Man-to-man defense may
be more difficult and take more time to master.
However, great players want that challenge.

PLAYING TOUGH DEFENSE

When a team is on the court, each of the five players plays both offense and defense. When on offense, a team tries to shoot the ball into the basket. When on defense, a team tries to stop the other team from scoring baskets. An offense runs plays to try and score points, and a defense runs plays to try to stop the other team from scoring. How an offense or defense plays together as a team determines who wins or loses the game.

When playing defense, there are two ways to play. You can play zone defense, or you can play man-to-man defense. A zone defense places the five players in specific spots on the floor. From these spots they guard the basket. The players don't move much. They wait for a pass to come to the area that they are

Playing tough defense means getting close to the ball handler.

guarding. This is their zone. If the ball doesn't come near their zone, the players don't do much playing at all. I don't see this as a very active style of basketball defense. Zone defense allows the offense to shoot too easily. There isn't a strong defense against the dribblers coming at the basket, either. Offensive players can get too close to the basket and shoot easily.

Man-to-man defense is a lot different. Here, the defensive player plays against one other player on the offense. He has other responsibilities, but mostly he guards that one "man" while playing defense. By having one player guard one other player, a man-to-man defense puts more pressure on the offense. Why? Because the offensive players are always being closely guarded. No offensive players are standing unguarded on the court. The defender is right against the body of the offensive player. The defender has his hands in the face of the offensive player. The defender is always trying to steal the ball or steal a pass. The defender is always trying to block a shot. There is a constant aggression toward getting the ball away from the offense. With this kind of defensive, you can see why it is better than a zone. Here's how the man-to-man defense can work for you.

THE DEFENSIVE TRANSITION

Defense begins the instant the opposing team takes away your team's control of the ball. This can happen because of a missed shot. It also can happen because the defense stole the ball. Maybe a pass was taken away. It doesn't matter how your offense lost control of the ball. As soon as it happens, your offense becomes your defense. This is called the transition. The offense changes over to the defense.

As soon as your offense loses the ball, you need to become a defender. This is defensive transition. You need to concentrate and become aggressive. Your focus is now on stopping your opponents.

Take Action

As a defender, you want to react quickly during the defensive transition. Don't waste time questioning a

Figure 1: During defensive transition, look back over your shoulder to see the ball.

referee's call or cheering a great play. Instead, turn and run to the other end of the court. Slow transition by any member of your team gives the opposing team a chance to score easily. As you run, look back over your shoulder to see the ball at all times (See Figure1). If you lose sight of the ball, change your body position until you can see it. You need to know where you should be on the court. To know this, you must know where the ball is, where your man is, and where the basket is.

Getting into Position

During defensive transition, you want to quickly run to the other end of the court. This gets you into position to guard your opponents. The three-point line is a good place for your teammates to be as your opponents come down the court with the ball. The three-point line is that long arcing line painted on the floor far from the basket. In fact, it's 19 feet 3 inches away from the basket. If your court has no three-point line, then set up outside the free-throw line.

At this point, any unguarded player must quickly be guarded. Talk to your teammates. If you are near the unguarded player, go and guard him. Tell a teammate to take your man. Talking to your teammates is key for good team defense.

GUARD YOUR MAN

Sometimes you will not need to guard an open player.

This is a good time to start defending your own man. You want to stay alert here. Stay with your man as the ball is passed from player to player. Your man might get the ball at any time.

Sometimes your team may be outnumbered close to the basket. This is the scoring area. Now you are not just responsible for your man. You may have to stop two or three players. Don't panic or you will let them score. Move quickly toward the ball handler. He is now your man. Make like you're going to lunge after the ball. You also can make like you're going to rush to him and block him with your body. These are fakes. Fakes are a good way to get a ball handler to pick up his dribble or pass sooner than he wants. If he does, you can defend against a pass.

Step back toward the basket and watch the other opponents. Now you are in the passing lane. Here you can block or steal a pass. Do anything you can to force an extra pass before an opponent can shoot. This allows time for your teammates to get back and help.

If an opponent clearly has an easy layup attempt,

do not foul from behind. Sometimes players miss lay-ups. Just make sure you hustle into position to rebound the missed shot.

Defense is a State of Mind

Anyone can learn to play basket-ball. Being a good defensive player is more than just being big and learning positioning. You must want to be a good defender. Wanting to play good defense requires desire, hustle, and energy.

DEFENDING ON THE BALL

When you are guarding an opponent who has the ball, you are playing "on ball" defense. This is the part of defensive play where your mistakes can hurt worst. Every player and fan will be able to see your man drive (dribble fast to the basket) past you to the basket. You've just been "burned." You weren't in position to stop him. Your man took advantage of this by moving around you quickly with his dribble. On ball defense needs your quickness and concentration.

DON'T REACT — ACT

The best way to play good defense is to act before your man acts. If your man quickly dribbles, or shoots, or passes, you can only react. However, if you get in your man's way, he can't dribble. If you have

Good defenders are ready to act against a ball handler.

your hands in his face, your man can't shoot. If you have your body against his and your arms up, he can't pass. This is acting. You always want to try to take away your man's best move. This can throw off his offensive rhythm. Forcing him to adjust to your defense may make him slower, unsure, and less confident. Make the ball handler react to you. Do not wait to react to his move. Try to force a turnover or a bad shot.

Know Your Opponent

1. How quick is he?
2. Does he like to drive to the basket?
3. How well does he use each hand to dribble and shoot?
4. Which shots or passes does he make best?
5. Is he selfish? (Does he hog the ball or force bad shots?)

Take and keep a position between your opponent and the basket. Wherever he takes the ball, be there with him. Don't foul, though.

Take a Stance

It's toughest to defend an opponent when he is dribbling. While dribbling, he has the ability to shoot, drive, or pass. He is a "triple threat" to the defense.

Position yourself at arm's length from the ball handler. Your stance should be comfortable. It should keep you balanced and allow you to move quickly in any direction. Your foot nearer the middle of the court should be slightly forward. Bend your knees. Make sure your butt is down low. Let your weight rest equally on the balls of your feet. Your feet should be spread shoulders' width apart. Arch your back slightly. Keep your head up and directly over the midpoint between your feet. This keeps you balanced. Now you're ready to move quickly. Keep your hands above your waist with your palms facing your man (See Figure 2, p. 18).

The Defensive Perimeter

The defensive perimeter is like the high fence around an army post. It is the first line of defense. In Diagram 1, a line drawn from X1 through X4 shows the defensive perimeter, or "shell." If a dribbler gets past one of these players, bad things can happen:

- The dribbler may get an uncontested shot.
- The dribbler now must be covered. This leaves an opposing player open to make a shot.
- To help cover the dribbler, defenders are taken out of good rebounding position.

Figure 2: Your stance gets you into position to guard any offensive player. Keep your hands up and out in front of you. Your knees should be bent so that you can move quickly.

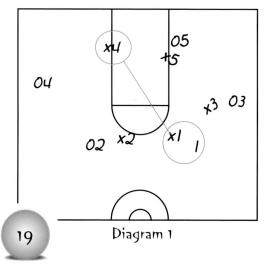

Diagram 1

Focus your eyes on your man's numbers (chest). I don't know anyone who can make a chest or belly fake. Do not concentrate on the ball. The ball is the first thing that can fake out a defender and leave him behind a driving opponent. Also, get the forward foot inside the ball handler (the side of him that's nearest the middle of the court). This position prevents a drive to the middle. Now your man can go only to the sideline or baseline. This is where you want to force him. He must now react to you.

FAKE FACTS

Smart players use fakes as they dribble. Getting the defender off balance or out of position allows him to take an open shot or drive by the defender. Reacting to fakes also leads to many fouls. The best thing you can do against a fake is to stay in your position. If the ball handler steps to the basket, step back quickly, pushing off your top foot. Then slide your top foot back into your stance. Stay balanced, shifting your weight to the back foot (See Figure 3).

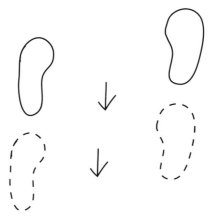

Figure 3: When the ball handler moves toward the basket, drop back with short steps to cut off his path.

On ball or shot fakes, never jump. This leaves you in the air while your man dribbles around you. Instead, stay on the floor until your man leaves his feet. Challenge any shot by jumping straight up with your arm extended. Keep your hand up and pointed to the ball. This puts a hand in the shooter's face. Now he can't see the basket well. Do not slap down at the ball. I also like defenders to yell at the shooter to break his concentration.

Time Out!

To be a good defender you must avoid these mistakes:

1. Don't allow ball handlers to dribble past you.
2. Don't be lazy or unaware in transition.
3. Don't react poorly to fakes.

BLOCKING SHOTS

Blocking shots is a big help to your team. A single blocked shot can change the energy of the game. Still, picking up a lot of fouls while trying to block every shot hurts your team.

When your man dribbles the ball, maintain your position with the slide step (See Figure 4). Make the first step a long one with the back foot. Then slide the top foot back to its normal position. You don't want

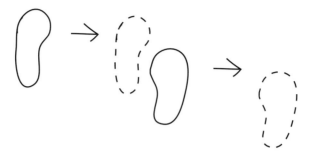

Figure 4: Following the dribbler requires you to slide step left or right. Make your steps short and quick to keep your balance.

to jump as you move. The idea is to slide your body using quick foot movement. While sliding, keep your outside hand up, waist-high, to defend against passes. Thrusting this hand in the direction you want to go helps to keep you moving smoothly. Hold your inside hand lower, closer to the ball handler's knees. If he tries to dribble back across to the other side of his body (a crossover dribble), you will be ready.

Wait for the dribbler to pick up the ball. Once the ball is picked up from a dribble, the ball handler can only pass or shoot. Now place your top foot between his legs and go belly-to-belly with him. This is called

Figure 5: When the ball handler picks up his dribble, get up close and place your knee between his legs. Raise your arms to trace the ball. You've just "put him in jail."

"putting him in jail" (See Figure 5). He'll have the ball over his head. Let your hands follow the ball. This is called tracing. Now you can call out "dead!" to your teammates. This lets them know they no longer have to watch the drive to the basket. They can increase the pressure on pass receivers.

If beaten by the dribbler, do not try to tip the ball from behind. Don't try to follow him, either. Turn to the middle of the court. Run toward the basket until you are ahead of the dribbler. Now get back into your defensive stance and keep sliding to force him toward either the sideline or the baseline. If the dribbler gets careless and has the ball in front of you, make him pay. Dig for the ball without changing your stance. Even if you do not steal the ball, you may upset the dribbler's rhythm. He might have to pick up his dribble.

Sometimes you will find yourself helping a teammate who's been driven backward by a dribbler. After helping him out, you will find yourself out of position. Your man may catch a pass when he is 10 to 20 feet away from you. You need to recover quickly. Run half the distance that you are away from your man. Then break down into your stance. Move forward with slide steps until you are in position to contest a shot or force the dribbler sideline or baseline. Now get closer with slide steps. You're now back to the best defensive position in which you can be.

DEFENDING AWAY FROM THE BALL

The key to defending a player without the ball is to keep moving. Move any time the ball is passed to another player. Move when your man moves. Make sure that you can stay close to your man but still be ready to help your teammates. You may have to help out if a pass is made to an open man who has moved quickly (cut) to the basket. This position is called a flat triangle. Always keep a flat triangle position between the ball, you, and your man (See Figure 6).

DEFENDING CUTS

When ten players are running on the court, it's easy for one to move quickly and get open on the court or near the basket. These quick moves are called cuts. To defend against cuts you have to be in a good position

Figure 6: Moving constantly is the key to man-to-man defense.

27

on the court. Your position on the court depends on how far your man is from the ball. Let's say he's one pass away. This means he is near enough to the ball handler to receive a pass. You now should be one step toward the basket off the passing lane, and about one-third of the distance to the ball. Your head should be in line with your opponent's inside shoulder. Stay down in a defensive stance with your top arm up and into the passing lane. This disrupts passes and sometimes lets you make a steal.

When your man moves, make sure you're in position to keep him from getting to the basket and receiving a pass. Do this by using good footwork (slide or drop steps). Keep your eyes on your man and the ball (See Figure 7).

Give-and-Go Cuts

Sometimes your man will make a pass and then cut toward the basket. He's hoping to get clear of you and get a pass back from the person to whom he passed the ball. This is called a "give-and-go" play. A

Figure 7: Good footwork keeps you between your man and the basket. Back steps and slide steps help you to move quickly.

give-and-go cut to the basket is tough to defend. Try this.

While the ball handler has the ball, you should be inside of him (toward the middle of the court). This position allows you to force him sideline and baseline. Once he passes the ball, you must get to the outside of him. Once outside of him, you will be

Figure 8: Defend a drib-bler by standing near the middle of the court.

Figure 9: When the ball is passed, move outside. This puts you between your defender and the ball.

between him and the ball. Now you can cut off his path to the basket. As the ball is passed, slide back two steps toward the ball. Never allow a cutter to get between you and the ball. (See Figures 8 and 9).

SCREENS

Screens happen when an offensive opponent who is away from the ball stands in a spot to block you from getting around him. This move frees your man to receive a pass and shoot uncontested.

Your man may become a screener either on or away from the ball. First, warn your teammate that a screen is coming. Tell him from where the screen is coming—right, left, or back. Be ready to help. Tell him to stay with his man or switch men with you.

FOUR

DEFENDING THE LOW POST

Every player should know how to defend the low post. The low post is that spot on both sides of the lane about 4 feet away from the basket. When your man receives a pass with his back to you at this spot, you are "posted up." This will happen to you often. It's part of the game, so don't panic. Some of the best low-post defenders are smaller than their opponents. Rather than depend on size, they use their brains, are aggressive, and use good footwork.

DENYING THE PASS

To deny a pass to the post man, try to get into a "three quarters' front" position. You want to have your top foot, shoulder, and arm in the passing lane.

Brian Grant (left) is a good low-post defender even though he is much smaller than many of the players he guards.

Your other hand feels or rests on, but does not hold, your man's back (See Figure 10).

Blocking the Post Man

When the ball is above the post man (nearer to the midcourt line), play on the midcourt side of him. This position is called the "high side." When the ball is passed to the post man on the baseline, play right behind him or toward the baseline. This position is called the "low side." Whatever position you need to be in to defend the post man, never lose sight of the ball. (See Figures 11 and 12, p. 36).

A good post man will try to keep you right behind him. By doing this, he can keep you from blocking a pass. He will try to get his top foot between your legs and pivot into you. You must win the "foot fight." Keep your top foot over the post man's. Get your top arm higher than his. Do not lean on your man. You can be called for a foul by leaning or pushing against your opponent. Use your footwork, not strength, to hold your position.

Figure 10: To deny a low-post pass, rest your arm on your opponent's back and keep your forward arm out in front of him.

Figure 11 (top): You can guard the low-post man by standing by his side. Figure 12 (bottom): You also can guard the low post man by standing in front of him. Either way, make sure you can see the ball at all times.

guard

Figure 13: Defending against the rebound requires you to go out to your man and block him from getting to the basket.

Defending Against the Rebound

Strong rebounding teams win a lot of games. Rebounds do not come easily. Nor do only the tallest players or the best jumpers grab rebounds. Strong rebounding depends on good position, timing, and aggressiveness.

Anticipate the shot. Find your man immediately. Don't wait to see where he is going. Go out to block

Figure 14: During the rebound, pivot to block your opponent from the ball and prepare yourself to get the rebound.

him as far from the basket as possible. Stop him from moving to the basket by bending your elbow and placing your forearm into his chest (See Figure 13, p. 37).

Pivot in the same direction as your opponent. Stay wide with your knees bent. Raise your arms and keep your elbows wide, with your fingers pointing up.

Figure 15: Pull the rebound down with two hands into your chest. Pivot away from your opponent to protect the ball.

Once the ball hits the rim, see in which direction it bounces and go get it (See Figure 14).

When you jump, extend both arms. Reach up and out to the ball. Grab the ball with both hands. Forcefully pull it down to your chest, keeping your elbows wide. Pivot away from your opponent to protect the ball (See Figure 15).

Most missed shots go off the rim to the opposite side from where the shot was taken. The longer the shot was, the longer the rebound will be. Help your team by getting to the right place at the right time. There is a saying in the NBA: "Rebounds get rings." Go get one!

If you work hard, you can be a good defender. Former NBA great Magic Johnson says great defense takes "practice, preparation, desire, and intensity." Practice will not always be fun. Take the challenge! Defend with intensity, intelligence, and controlled aggression. Dominate your opponent. Help your team win!

Magic Johnson (left) says great defense takes "practice, preparation, desire, and intensity."

NEW WORDS

contest to attempt to interfere with a shot

cover moving to guard an open man who has beaten his man

crossover dribble a move by which the dribbler changes direction by dribbling the ball across the front of his body; or, footwork through which the ball handler changes direction by stepping across his body while keeping the pivot foot down

drive dribbling the ball toward the basket in an attempt to beat the defender

flat triangle position a position where a defender is close to his man but still able to help other players

give-and-go after passing, a player makes a cut to the basket looking for a return pass

passing lane in the area of the block, an offensive player's attempt to gain a position to receive a pass

screen a legal offensive maneuver by which a player takes away the path of a defender. Also called a pick

switch a maneuver in which two defenders trade responsibilities for the men they are assigned to guard

three-quarter front a defender has one arm, shoulder, and foot between the ball and a man posted up

triple-threat the ball handler has the ball in front of his shooting shoulder and is in position to shoot, drive, or pass

FOR FURTHER READING

Goldstein, Sidney. *The Basketball Shooting Guide.* Philadelphia: Golden Aura, 1998.

Lieberman-Cline, Nancy, et al. *Basketball for Women: Becoming a Complete Player.* Champaign, IL: Human Kinetics, 1995.

McCarthy, Jr., John P. *Youth Basketball, 2nd ed.* Cincinnati, OH: Betterway Books, 1996.

Mikes, Jay, and Ray Meyer. *Basketball FundaMENTALS: A Complete Mental Training Guide.* Champaign, IL: Human Kinetics, 1995.

St. Martin, Ted, and Frank Frangie. *The Art of Shooting Baskets: From Free Throws to the Slam Dunk.* Lincolnwood, IL: NTC Contemporary, 1992.

RESOURCES

American Youth Basketball Tour

www.aybtour.com

2150 Anderson SE

E. Grand Rapids, MI 49506

(800) 685-7194 ext. 6762

Web Sites

Women's National Basketball Association

http://wnba.com/

Get all the breaking news of the Women's National Basketball Association at this site. There are also player profiles available for you to research, and playing tips from the pros.

National Basketball Association

http://nba.com/

The National Basketball Association's own Web site gives you up-to-the-minute news about all things having to do with the NBA. Included are news articles that offer fans detailed reports about the teams and players around the league.

National College Athletic Association (NCAA)
http://ncaa.org/
Find school team schedules and view stats of your favorite teams and players. The NCAA online site is not just for fans, though. Learn about college basketball scholarship awards!

INDEX

About the Author

Bill Van Gundy has coached on the high school and college levels for 41 years. His teams are known for their aggressive man-to-man defense and disciplined offense. He frequently speaks at clinics and summer camps and has had fifteen articles published. Coach Van Gundy is the father of Stan, the assistant head coach of the Miami Heat, and Jeff, the head coach of the New York Knickerbockers.